Priest

"Metal Gods"

Brian J. Bowe

Judas Priest (from left to right: Glenn Tipton, K.K. Downing, Rob Halford, Dave Holland, and Ian Hill) performed at the

1

HEAVY METAL SUNDAY

It is a scene that has been repeated over and over for four decades. It begins with a thunderous wall of sound—a sound so thick the air felt like a substance that could be touched. Five men dressed in black leather take the stage, silver studs sparkling. With drums pounding and guitars blazing, the band launches into its powerful performance.

The audience members, as sweaty as the athletic band members they came to watch, pump their fists and sing along to the muscular sound. It's an exchange of energy that grows larger and larger—the band incites the fans, the fans respond with devotion, until it reaches an explosive peak. If the band has its uniform, so do the fans—

long hair, black t-shirts, and leather wristbands are the style. Together, the band and fans form a united front, and for a brief moment, all the stress and loneliness of the outside world is held at bay.

Even though it was an oft-repeated scene, this particular concert was an important one for British heavy metal band Judas Priest. Standing on stage in front of a half million people at the US Festival on May 29, 1983, Judas Priest frontman Rob Halford sang the words, "I'm on the top as long as the music's loud." Those lyrics—from the band's rebellious hit single "You've Got Another Thing Comin'"—captured what was happening for the band.

At that moment, the music was loud and Halford and his bandmates were on top. After ten years of constant recording and touring, the band had finally reached superstar status around the world. And with the US Festival appearance, Judas Priest found itself at the crest of a pop culture wave. Held in San Bernardino, California, the US Festival was founded by Apple Computer co-founder Steve Wozniak in an attempt to combine rock 'n' roll music with cutting-edge computer technology. Nineteen eighty-three was the festival's second—and final—year.

But one of the most notable events of the 1983 festival had nothing to do with computers. Much attention that year was given to Heavy Metal Sunday. Featuring Judas Priest, Ozzy Osbourne, Mötley Crüe, Quiet Riot, Triumph, the

Scorpions, and Van Halen, the event is credited with rekindling popular interest in the genre of heavy metal, which had fallen out of favor.

"It was the day that new wave died and rock and roll took over," wrote Mötley Crüe singer Vince Neil.[1]

Judas Priest had released its breakthrough album *Screaming for Vengeance* the year before and was at the end of a major tour. The band was at the peak of its creativity and popularity. Little did they know that within a few short years, they would face challenges that would land them in court and threaten the band's existence.

Heavy metal has always been an art form with a bad reputation among some people. It is an aggressive style of music that features loud and distorted guitars, powerful vocals, and hammering drums. In its early days (and even now), many parents and other adults didn't understand it and complained about it. But for the masses of devoted metal fans (often called "headbangers"), heavy metal provides a release for day-to-day frustrations and a sense of community with fellow fans.

Judas Priest didn't invent heavy metal. Some people say that Black Sabbath or Led Zeppelin invented it. Others say the heavy feedback-drenched hippie bands, such as Blue Cheer and Iron Butterfly created it. Still others trace its beginnings to the reference to "heavy metal thunder" in the band Steppenwolf's motorcycle anthem "Born To Be Wild."

But whoever invented it, there's no question that Judas Priest perfected it.

Judas Priest was the first metal band to popularize wearing black leather and studs onstage. The dual-lead guitar sound of Glenn Tipton and K.K. Downing would become standard for metal bands in years to come. Rob Halford's high, operatic vocals have been imitated by many metal singers. His lyrics dealing with dark themes and encouraging people to stand up for themselves and fight authority are also classic metal.

"One of the cool things about Priest is that we're commonly known as the originators of the look, the image," said Halford.[2]

The band's influence is wide-ranging. Judas Priest "set the stage for every Eighties band from Mötley Crüe to Metallica," wrote *Rolling Stone*'s Rob Kemp.[3] Twisted Sister singer Dee Snider said, "Judas Priest was the first band to take heavy metal and embrace it as a term and as a music form."[4]

Onstage at the US Festival, the band's constant creative core—singer Halford, guitarists Downing and Tipton, and bassist Ian Hill—had come a long way from their hard, working-class British upbringing. But that upbringing helped inspire much of the band's trademark look and sound. The leather-and-studs look combined with Halford's powerful screams and the twin guitar attack of Downing and Tipton

THE US FESTIVAL DREW THOUSANDS OF PEOPLE.

didn't just define Judas Priest, it set the model for heavy metal bands everywhere.

"With its exaggerated leather-'n'-studs theatrical bent and polished musical consistency, Judas Priest encapsulates the metal experience for true believers," wrote Mark Coleman and Steve Appleford in *The New Rolling Stone Album Guide*.[5]

Halford agreed with the band's importance to the heavy metal genre.

"This is the first true original heavy metal band in existence," Halford said. "It's as important as when Bob Dylan walks out on stage, when the Rolling Stones walk out on stage—Judas Priest carries that on its shoulders."[6]

One of the things that has made Judas Priest's popularity last is that the band's sound is always evolving, even while staying true to its metal roots.

Heavy metal journalist Geoff Barton wrote that Judas Priest has "constantly reinvented themselves over the years. That's not to say they've altered their direction dramatically— rather they've looked at musical trends and studied the mood of society in general, and where appropriate they've incorporated relevant aspects into their style of music."[7]

Halford remains proud of the band's accomplishments. "You can't ask for more than to be remembered as one of the greatest British heavy metal bands of all time," Halford said.[8]

To fully understand Judas Priest, travel to the rough and gritty streets of Birmingham, England. But first, look at the men who make up the band.

2

WHO IS JUDAS PRIEST?

The main core of Judas Priest is singer Rob Halford, guitarists K.K. Downing and Glenn Tipton, and bassist Ian Hill. Those four members were constant through the band's rise to stardom. The band has featured several drummers, and when Halford left the band from 1992 to 2003, he was replaced by a singer named Tim "Ripper" Owens.

Rob Halford

The most recognizable member of Judas Priest is most likely frontman Rob Halford. As the band's voice, lyricist, and creator of its look, for many he is the face of the group.

Halford was born in 1951 in Walsall, England. As a youngster, he was a fan of

JUDAS PRIEST IN THE EARLY 1970s

American western TV shows, such as *The Lone Ranger* and *The Cisco Kid*.[1]

From a young age, Halford was drawn to singing and performing in front of people.

"When I was in my early grades at school, I was able to get into the school choir and be a part of all of the school productions. I just ran to that," Halford said. "It made me feel good inside. Everybody likes to be looked at and applauded, especially when you're a child. I think that stuck with me."[2]

As a youth, he was interested in writing, according to his sister.

Rob Halford
in 1979

"He was always writing words down, poetry, and we just always figured he was going to do something out of the ordinary," said Halford's sister Sue.[3]

Halford also carried a burden inside. By the time he was in his teens, Halford knew he was homosexual. Being gay wasn't accepted in England in those days, so he kept it a secret. "When he was a teenager, Rob hid the fact. It must have been a very, very difficult time for him," said Sue.[4]

Halford felt like such an outsider that he quit school.

"I left school at 16 and went straight to work for a large theater," Halford said. "I went from those high-school experiences in the straight world to the theater with gay men everywhere. I started to mix with my own kind, and I started to feel as though I wasn't the only one."[5]

Halford also found a release from his feelings of loneliness by turning to rock and roll.

"It's an awful feeling of being lost and confused and alone. Because, when you're a teenager especially, you don't know where to go and who to talk to," Halford said. "Music is, at that point, your only friend."[6]

K.K. Downing

One of the two remaining founders of Judas Priest, guitarist Kenneth "K.K." Downing was born in 1951 in West Bromwich, England.[7]

K.K. Downing in 1983

Downing's early years were rough. His family was poor, and his parents didn't support his desire to play guitar. Eventually, they kicked him out of the house.[8]

"A lot of kids out there have problems with their parents. I know I did," Downing told *Kerrang!* magazine in the mid-1980s. "I got kicked out of the house when I was 16 and I haven't spoken to my folks since."[9]

He quit school, left home, and took a job as an apprentice chef in a hotel. He liked the work, but soon the guitar called out to him.

"It was a great job but then I had a ten day holiday so I took that to go and see Jimi Hendrix play at Woburn Abbey. I was so amazed by that that the ten days turned into six weeks because I then went abroad to see some other festivals," Downing said.[10]

Downing began playing guitar when he was sixteen years old, inspired by guitarists like Hendrix, John Mayall, and Eric Clapton. "I had a couple of classical lessons, but couldn't afford to keep them up so I just got on with the metal," Downing said.[11]

Glenn Tipton

The other half of Judas Priest's twin-lead guitar attack, Glenn Tipton was born October 25, 1949, in Blackheath, England. He was surrounded by music because his mother was a pianist

Glenn Tipton
in 1986

and his brother played guitar. However, Tipton himself didn't start playing until he was a young adult.[12]

"I started out myself rather late," Tipton said. "I was 18. Most kids start when they are about 10 or 11 and they live that life ever since. I never took a lesson until I was 20, and I'm glad I had those years living the life of a normal person. I don't consider that time wasted."[13]

Even though he got a late start, once he began he was enthusiastic about his new craft.

"I was a bit of a late bloomer," he said, "but once I started, I was totally absorbed. I never put the guitar down in those days. I gave dedication a completely new meaning."[14]

Part of his devotion to the guitar came from what Tipton was doing with his life—working for the British Steel Company. It was a job that he didn't want.

"I worked in a factory for five years, and boy, I wasn't wanting that," Tipton said. "Really, that was the order of events—just trying to do something with my life. I just saw music as an option. My mother was a pianist and my brother played guitar, so that's just the way it went."[15]

Tipton is married and has two children. He said that being separated from his family is the hardest part of life as a rock star.[16]

"It's taken away time from my family," Tipton said. "That's been the biggest sacrifice—just being away from home. You do what you've got to do though, and we're really lucky to do this and have a fan base that's very loyal. We are lucky to be in Judas Priest and have fans as enthusiastic as they are. There probably isn't one day where I don't turn around and say just how happy I am with my situation in life."[17]

Ian Hill

Even though he's not usually in the limelight, bassist Ian Hill was one of the founders of Judas Priest, along with Downing.

He learned how to play bass from his father, who died when Hill was fifteen.

"[M]y father played double bass in jazz bands, he was the one who taught me rudiments of the bass," Hill said.[18]

Hill met Downing when the two went to the same school.

"We have known each other since we were five," Hill said. "We were brought up in the same housing estate just outside of Birmingham. We weren't really friends until we were about 15 or 16 and first started to get into

IAN HILL IN THE 1980s

music. We were into progressive rock, which in those days was Cream, Jimi Hendrix, John Mayall & The Bluesbreakers and Fleetwood Mac. We had very, very similar tastes in music."[19]

Hill married Rob Halford's sister Sue, and they have a son named Alexander. They divorced in 1988. Hill now has a daughter with his second wife.[20]

Tim "Ripper" Owens

When Rob Halford quit Judas Priest in 1992, American singer Tim Owens was hired to take his place in the band. It was a dream come true for Owens, who had long been a metal fan.

Owens was born September 13, 1967, near Akron, Ohio. When he was sixteen years old, his older brother bought the Judas Priest album *Screaming for Vengeance*. He became such a fan that for his eighteenth birthday, his cake had the Metallian, a robot beast from the cover of the *Defenders of the Faith* album on it.[21]

Growing up, he loved heavy metal, and he loved to sing. He was a member of his high school's madrigal choir, singing a type of unaccompanied classical vocal music. But he also spent time singing in metal bands—including a Judas Priest tribute band called British Steel.[22]

Drummers

Judas Priest has had eight drummers over the years. In the early years, John Ellis, Alan Moore, Chris Campbell, John

Hinch, Simon Phillips, and Les Binks played short stints with the band.

The group's sixth drummer, Dave Holland, was born April 5, 1948, in Northamptonshire, Wolverhampton, England.[23] Holland joined Judas Priest in 1979—just in time for the recording of the groundbreaking *British Steel* album. He had previously played with a band called Trapeze. He is the second-longest-serving drummer for the band. Holland left after the *Ram It Down* album in 1989.

"I think Dave would probably be the first to admit that heavy metal was . . . *important* to him, but maybe not as important as it is to someone like me, who lives, breathes, drinks, sleeps, eats heavy metal music," Halford said. "He made a professional and a gentleman decision by leaving the group."[24]

In 2004, Holland was convicted of sexually assaulting a seventeen-year-old boy who had been taking drum lessons from him.[25] He was sentenced to eight years in prison.[26]

Holland was replaced by Racer X drummer Scott Travis in 1990. Travis is the band's current drummer. He is the longest-serving drummer the band has ever had.

Travis was born September 6, 1961, in Norfolk, Virginia.[27] He was attracted to the drums at a young age.

"I just saw the drum set itself and thought, 'hey man, that looks like a cool instrument,' with all the chrome parts and things like that. I don't know if anyone has a clear, definite reason why they start playing a particular instrument. It's just something that they're drawn to."[28]

His main influences are Ringo Starr from the Beatles, Ian Paice from Deep Purple, John Bonham from Led Zeppelin, Alex Van Halen from Van Halen, and Neil Peart from Rush.[29]

Travis was the first American member of Judas Priest, which is a very British band. Halford said Travis's nationality didn't bother him.

"It doesn't matter to me that Scott's an American," Halford said. "He could have been Swedish, he could have been French, he could have been from Holland, it doesn't matter. It's the quality of the work that matters, and he was the best heavy metal drummer we could find."[30]

3

BRITISH STEEL

The story of Judas Priest began on the gritty industrial streets of England's second largest city, Birmingham. The city was filled with large factories and mills. It was a loud and dirty place, and the people who worked in those factories did hard jobs. That tough, high-energy way of life made the working-class people who lived there crave high-energy entertainment. By the end of the 1960s, the city gave birth to the style of music known as heavy metal.

Located in a part of England known as the Midlands, Birmingham is a manufacturing town. In fact, it was the birthplace of the Industrial Revolution.

BIRMINGHAM, ENGLAND, WAS KNOWN AS A MANUFACTURING TOWN. THIS PHOTO WAS TAKEN IN THE 1960s.

The Industrial Revolution began in 1769, when inventor Richard Arkwright introduced a new machine for spinning cotton into thread. That same year, another inventor, James Watt, perfected the steam engine, which Arkwright used to power his new machine.[1]

Before that time, people had to spin thread and weave cloth at home. Using steam to power machines meant that factories no longer needed to be built next to rivers to supply power. They could be built anywhere. Towns sprang up around the factories. These new factories could run around the clock, and people began working in shifts.[2]

This new breed of factory was described as "a house of horrors, economically, physically and mentally."[3] Low pay meant entire families had to work long hours—even the children. Dust and pollution inside the factories caused breathing diseases. The machines sometimes cut off arms and legs.[4]

It was a bleak life. Historian Sean Lang wrote:

> The factory owner built the workers' houses, which were cheap and cramped, with no sanitation. Workers used a factory shop, where they paid with tokens provided by the factory. Children worked in the factory, crawling in and out beneath the moving machinery. If you tried to set up a trade union you'd be out of a job. And if you went on strike, what would you live on? No strike pay existed, and no unemployment benefit either.[5]

Even though life was hard, people began flocking to cities to work in the factories. "All those inventions had created two new classes of people, the factory owners and the factory workers, and the workers were discovering just how powerful the owners really were," Lang wrote.[6]

Along with factories for making cloth, Birmingham also had access to the raw materials for making steel. The city continued as an industrial center through the 1800s and into the 1900s.

During World War II, Birmingham's industrial importance made it a target. Germany hit Birmingham hard during a bombing known as the Blitz (from the German word *Blitzkrieg*, which means "lightning war"). During the Blitz, the Germans dropped 1,852 tons of bombs on Birmingham.[7]

Birmingham's industrial base and wartime ruin influenced the city's culture—so much so that the city is defined as much by the heavy metal music that it has produced as it is with the real metal produced by companies, such as British Steel. The children who were born during World War II and in the years right after it ended in 1945 were also the first children to grow up in the rock and roll era.

Two of the bands considered innovators of heavy metal—Black Sabbath and Judas Priest—come from Birmingham. Many Birmingham heavy metal musicians remember the hard life caused by the factories and the aftereffects of the war. The bleak surroundings helped influence the doom-and-gloom sound of metal.

"In the second world war in Birmingham, that's where all the ammunition was made. That's why it got so heavily bombed," said Black Sabbath bassist Geezer Butler. "There were all these bricks all over the place and bombed out buildings and all that kind of stuff."[8]

Black Sabbath is considered by many to be the first heavy metal band. Formed in Birmingham in 1968, they were the first band to combine the giant guitar riffs, thick bass lines, pounding drums, and evil-sounding lyrics that are the defining traits of metal music.

Birmingham's industry had a direct influence on Black Sabbath's sound. Guitarist Tony Iommi was working in a sheet metal factory and cut the ends of two fingers on his left hand off in an accident. He overcame his disability by inventing his own kind of false fingertips. He tuned his guitar down to a lower pitch to make it easier to play, which contributed to the thick sound that is characteristic of heavy metal.[9]

"It just gave us a great feeling of 'this is what we're about,'" said Iommi. "We liked the idea of those evilly sounding riffs."[10]

Birmingham influenced Black Sabbath in other ways. "I hated it, living there," said Iommi. "I think that influenced our music, as far as where we come from and the area we were from. It made it sort of more mean."[11]

Black Sabbath's self-titled first album and second album *Paranoid* featured spine-chilling songs about the devil, war, and drugs. Singer Ozzy Osbourne's stage presence and outrageous behavior set the standard for the metal singers who followed.

Even though both bands were from Birmingham, Hill said there never was competition between Black Sabbath and

Judas Priest. "They had already made their mark," he said. "We didn't want to sound like them and they didn't want to sound like us."[12]

There were other heavy British bands at the time—notably Deep Purple, Led Zeppelin, Uriah Heep, and UFO. American bands, such as the Stooges, the MC5, Iron Butterfly, Grand Funk Railroad, and Blue Cheer were also expanding the limits of heavy music. This first wave of heavy rock was still rooted in American blues-based rock and roll, influenced by African-American music from Chicago and the Mississippi Delta. Some of those bands could be called heavy metal, but there's no question that Black Sabbath and Judas Priest played an important role in turning heavy metal into its own genre of music, with brutal volume, dark lyrics, and a thick, gloomy sound.

"The roots of metal are very definitely within Priest and Sabbath," said Halford.[13]

Scott Ian, a guitarist with the metal band Anthrax, agreed. "As much as Sabbath started it, Priest were the ones who took it out of the blues and straight into metal. They were the first ones that were all metal all the time," said Ian.[14]

Judas Priest singer Halford remembered the factories having an impact on his education.

"I remember as a kid being in class, and next door to the school was one of these big metal foundries," said Halford. "You'd be in class trying to study and you could actually hear the metal hammers and the compressors banging and spitting forth metal and all this smoke, and it was drifting into the classroom and the books on the desk would be bouncing. You could actually physically feel it. I sometimes think that's the culprit. I actually breathed that metal into my lungs. It got into my blood."[15]

In fact, Halford later talked about how heavy metal is a particularly British type of music.

"[T]o me, the true definition of heavy metal comes from England," Halford said. "There are some good imitators elsewhere, but there's no way they can sound like a heavy metal band! The whole approach to the instruments is a lot more aggressive and a lot more powerful."[16] Halford said:

> I think that's why there are so many good bands from Birmingham, why heavy metal came from the Midlands. If you live in a council house (housing project) on a really bleak estate—where I'm from—and you look out the window every morning, you think 'God, there must be something better than this!' And you just take whatever God-given talents and abilities you've got and you use them to get out.
>
> Fortunately for me, I could sing and write songs. It took a while, but I'm glad to say I made it.[17]

For some of the budding band members of Birmingham, the potential of hard life in a factory provided powerful inspiration to pursue music. In fact, Tipton points to his firsthand

TEENS LOOK FOR THEIR FAVORITE ARTISTS IN A RECORD SHOP IN THE 1960s.

factory experience as one of the reasons he decided to become a musician.

While rock and roll was invented in America, by the 1960s the British were starting to perfect their own version of it. Bands, such as the Beatles, the Rolling Stones, and the Kinks took the blues and rock from the United States and turned up the energy to create something new. American guitarist Jimi Hendrix moved to England and created an outlandish kind of psychedelic music that featured loud guitar feedback and strange noises. (Psychedelic music became popular in the 1960s around the same time as the drug LSD, which causes hallucinations. Psychedelic music is meant to mimic the hallucinations of LSD.) The fiery guitar work of Hendrix and the British band Cream appealed to Birmingham youths who were used to hearing the loud sounds of the factories.

"Hendrix was my idol," said Downing. "I don't think there's ever going to be anyone else quite like him."[18]

Though he was an American, Hendrix spent much of his time living in England, and that's where he first became famous. When Hendrix died of a drug overdose in 1970, Downing and schoolmate Hill were both upset—and inspired to make their own music.

"We just bumped into each other one day and started talking about music. We found out that we were both into Cream, Hendrix and John Mayall, so we decided to get our own group together," Hill said.[19]

Hill and Downing were looking for a singer when they teamed up with Al Atkins. Atkins had been in a previous band called Judas Priest, but that original band had none of the same members as the group that became famous later. The name came from a Bob Dylan song called "The Ballad of Frankie Lee and Judas Priest," and Atkins's new group decided to recycle the name Judas Priest. With drummer John Ellis, Judas Priest began playing shows around the Midlands. Over the next two years, Ellis left and was replaced by Alan Moore, who was replaced by Chris Campbell.[20]

There was an active music scene in Birmingham at that time. "It was a strange situation in the area where we were at the time," said Hill. "There was a nucleus of probably 20 pretty good musicians and vocalists. And they all formed these groups. And, Judas Priest was one of those—and it was one of the better ones."[21]

Playing music may have offered the promise of a life away from working in a factory, but life as a musician wasn't easy for the members of Judas Priest in the early days.

Jimi Hendrix (left) was a big influence to many musicians in the 1960s.

"There were many times when we played just to get enough money to feed ourselves and buy some new guitar strings. It was really a day-to-day existence. Heavy metal wasn't exactly the rage in the early Seventies, and we had a lot of people to convince," Tipton said.[22]

The fact that the members of Judas Priest came from difficult circumstances helped them relate to their fans.

"These people didn't come from affluent backgrounds, and therefore they grew up and knew exactly how to present their music to people who came from a like-minded situation," said music journalist Malcolm Dome.[23]

Unhappy with the band's poverty, Atkins and Campbell left Judas Priest in 1973.

"It was a very difficult time. I didn't think the band was going to actually make it, believe it or not," Atkins said years later. "I thought, we'd been doing this for, what, two or three years now with this lineup, so I sort of decided in the end to call it a day."[24]

Ian Hill's girlfriend (and later wife) Sue Halford suggested her brother Rob might be a good replacement for Atkins.

"I went over to K.K. and Ian's place, which was an apartment just outside Birmingham, and I sat in the bedroom with them for a couple of hours, talking about music and different things. Since they were also checking out drummers, I suggested bringing in John Hinch, who had been in my previous band Hiroshima," Halford said.[25]

In 1974, the band signed to Gull Records and added a second guitarist, Glenn Tipton from a group called The Flying Hat Band. With Tipton's addition to the band, the core of the group was set. Judas Priest now had a unique two-guitar attack that would come to define the thick sound of heavy metal.

"Overnight, it gave the band a lot more depth and a lot more versatility," Tipton said.[26]

The band recorded its debut album, *Rocka Rolla*, in 1974 with Black Sabbath producer Roger Bain. The record was

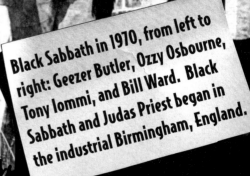

Black Sabbath in 1970, from left to right: Geezer Butler, Ozzy Osbourne, Tony Iommi, and Bill Ward. Black Sabbath and Judas Priest began in the industrial Birmingham, England.

recorded on a low budget, and the sound was bluesier than the heavy metal Judas Priest would eventually be known for.

"We had absolutely no money whatsoever," said Downing. "I remember everything being very rushed because we were in a good studio, but the budget was so tight we just ran out of money."[27]

Because of the rushed schedule, the band didn't like the way the album turned out.

"It was the production on *Rocka Rolla* that was the problem," Hill said. "It was a pity as the material really was good and the performances were good but the production laid down terribly."[28]

In April 1975, Judas Priest made its television debut on the British Broadcasting Company's show *The Old Grey Whistle Test*. In that footage, the band looks very different from how it would look in later years. There was no leather or studs—instead the band wore bell-bottomed trousers. Downing wore a wide-brimmed hat that hid his face. Halford wore a soft and silky blouse and sported shoulder-length hair.

Playing the songs "Rocka Rolla" and "Dreamer Deciever/Deciever," the band's sound wasn't as heavy as it would become. The double-guitar assault of Tipton and Downing and Halford's high screams were there. And the band was loud—the show's soundmen put carpets over Judas Priest's speaker cabinets and put up a sign that said, "Get your earplugs here."[29]

Judas Priest released *Sad Wings of Destiny* in 1976. That album was a great improvement over *Rocka Rolla*. The band's sound was starting to come together, and the album featured several songs that have become Priest classics, including "Victim of Changes" and "The Ripper."

"We were all getting more professional. It shows to a huge degree on the second album. It wasn't just the production, it was the performances themselves too," Hill said.[30]

Judas Priest toured throughout England and started to develop a devoted following of fans.

"On stage, it must be said, we just let rip. The Judas Priest machine rolls into town and the fans will always have a night to remember," Tipton told journalist Geoff Barton at the time.[31]

Even though *Sad Wings of Destiny* received good reviews, the band was still having a hard time making a living. The future looked bleak for Judas Priest, as British music fans were starting to listen to a new kind of music—punk rock. But the band's luck changed when it signed to Columbia Records in the United States.

UNLEASHED

4

By 1976, the first wave of heavy metal—including bands, such as Black Sabbath and Deep Purple— was starting to lose popularity, thanks to changing musical trends. In England, the new popular form of music was punk rock, and bands, such as the Sex Pistols and the Clash were getting a lot of attention.

"Metal almost fizzled out around the punk/new wave era," said Halford.[1]

Geoff Barton, the founding editor of *Kerrang!* magazine said that punk's status helped change heavy metal. "To a large part, it destroyed heavy metal in the U.K. Ultimately I think it forced it to recreate itself," he said.[2]

JUDAS PRIEST GOT TO PLAY WITH LED ZEPPELIN AND
OTHER BANDS DURING THE 1977 DAY ON THE GREEN
FESTIVAL IN OAKLAND, CALIFORNIA.

In the United States, punk was popular, but disco music was even bigger during this period. But even as different styles of music were selling more, Judas Priest stayed true to its metal roots.

"You had to kind of chisel out your own image and sound," said Downing.[3]

After signing with Columbia, Judas Priest went into the studio to record *Sin After Sin* in 1977. Deep Purple bassist Roger Glover produced the album after a recommendation by the record company.

The album contains two live staples of Judas Priest's stage show, "Sinner" and a cover of "Diamonds and Rust," a song written by folksinger Joan Baez about her romantic relationship with fellow singer Bob Dylan.

They brought in a new drummer named Simon Phillips for the sessions. Drummer Les Binks replaced Phillips on the following tour, which brought Judas Priest to the United States for the first time. Judas Priest was the opening act for softer rock bands, REO Speedwagon and Foreigner. The high point of the tour was opening for Led Zeppelin at the Day on the Green festival in Oakland, California, playing in front of 120,000 people over two days. The band credits this festival with helping make it popular in the western part of the United States.[4]

LED ZEPPELIN'S LEAD SINGER ROBERT PLANT SINGS AT THE DAY ON THE GREEN FESTIVAL.

After the *Sin After Sin* tour, Judas Priest went back into the studio and began recording the *Stained Class* album.

Stained Class was released in 1978. Judas Priest went out on a world tour that included Europe, Japan, and the United States. They played American dates as part of a triple bill with two other bands: Angel, and the Godz. Legendary *New York Times* music critic Robert Palmer saw a performance at the Palladium in March 1978. In his review, Palmer was not impressed.

"Judas Priest concentrates on putting over lyrics, a rare thing in heavy metal, but the lyrics, which revolve around ponderous themes such as sin and death, are not very profound," he wrote.[5]

At this time, the band began to change the way it dressed onstage. They began to move away from satin blouses, bell-bottom pants, and wide-brimmed hats. They began to wear black leather and metal studs because it seemed to fit with the music they were playing.[6]

In *Trouser Press* magazine, writer Jon Young noted Halford's stage wardrobe—close cropped hair and leather and studs. "Before we do any tour we sit back and design our own clothes. I felt that this particular outfit was what this particular tour needed, an aggressive severe very dominating type of role," Halford said.[7]

Young was impressed with Judas Priest's live show. "Their act was so powerful, so immediate, that I soon didn't care whether they were in tune or that the volume made me feel like I was being hit over the head with a bag of wet sand. And JP's lack of posturing made the other two bands [Angel and the Godz], both of whom rely on various contrivances to put their music across, look silly and weak by comparison."[8]

In an interview, Tipton talked to Young about the band's straightforward approach. "We don't mess around, we just play rock," Tipton said. He explained:

> I think a lot of rock bands try to be a bit too clever. We
> don't. If we get off on it, there's no way the kids can sit
> there and not get off on it as well. When we're jumpin'
> about on stage or banging out a riff, we feel it as much
> as the kids do. We enjoy what we're doing and that's the
> secret of Judas Priest. We go out there and just totally
> believe in what we're doing. We don't even totally believe
> in it, we're just doing what comes naturally. It's raw and
> that's gonna be the secret of our success. That's the
> attraction to a lot of kids. They can relate to us musically
> and lyrically and in general.[9]

Heavy metal still seemed like it was dying off in 1979. But thanks to its energetic live shows, Judas Priest's fan base was growing. And with its next album, the band would change the look of heavy metal forever.

Judas Priest released *Hell Bent for Leather* in 1979 (titled *Killing Machine* in Great Britain). The motorcycle song "Hell Bent for Leather" inspired Halford and helped perfect the band's look, which included leather, studs, handcuffs, and whips.

"For a number of the early formative years of metal, the image was not tied into the fierceness and the strength and power of the music," Halford said. "We didn't really nail it down, so to speak, until we brought about that song and started to explore this territory. It made absolute sense."[10]

The new stage outfits were the last piece of the puzzle for the band.

"We had all this great sound, we had the show we had the lights. We had all these great things going on. But there was just something just not connecting from the visual perspective," Halford said.[11]

Halford was the first one to take up the look, but soon the entire band adopted it.

"We never sat down and said 'let's all wear leather.' We fell into it. I think Rob was the first, and then gradually we all started to wear leather, and it seemed so right," said Tipton.[12]

After Judas Priest refined the heavy metal look, many other bands embraced it. "It became a kind of a uniform," Halford said. "If you looked at a band's photo, you knew they were metal because of all this, and the chains and studs. That's a metal band."[13]

To support *Hell Bent for Leather*, Judas Priest went out on another world tour—including its first headlining tour of the United States. On this 1979 tour, Halford introduced one of his trademark stage moves—riding onstage on a Harley-Davidson motorcycle during the album's title song.

"Priest presents itself as larger-than-life outlaw heroes on the run through a hostile, demon-riddled universe," wrote *Los Angeles Times* reviewer Don Snowden after a concert in Santa Monica, California. "The music is delivered with split-second precision and follows a simple formula, built around the heavy riffing of guitarists K.K. Downing and Glen[n] Tipton and topped by Halford's high-pitched singing and piercing shrieks."[14]

By the late 1970s, Judas Priest started to change their look. They were now wearing leather and studs. On tour, Rob Halford would ride a Harley-Davidson motorcycle on stage.

Judas Priest played a series of dates in Japan on this tour, and those shows were recorded for a live album called *Unleashed in the East*, which was released in 1979. It marked the first time the band worked with producer Tom Allom. The album was mixed at Startling Studios in the British countryside. That studio was located in a mansion called Tittenhurst Park, which was owned by Beatles drummer Ringo Starr. Starr bought it from fellow Beatle John Lennon.[15]

"I don't think we were totally aware of the history behind the house or the studio at all," said Downing.[16]

After the *Hell Bent for Leather* tour, a new drummer named Dave Holland replaced Les Binks. Holland came from the British city of Northampton and had played in a band called Trapeze with bassist and singer Glen Hughes, who later performed with both Deep Purple and Black Sabbath.

Many people consider Judas Priest's next album, 1980's *British Steel*, to be one of the best metal records of all time. To record it, the band returned to Tittenhurst Park with producer Tom Allom for four weeks. The band wasn't finished writing the songs for the album when they went into the studio, but they were inspired by the surroundings to write there. Classic Priest songs like "Living After Midnight," "Breakin' the Law," and "The Rage" were written there.[17]

"We started setting up in the studio, which was very small and very dead, and within a matter of a few hours we realized that we simply weren't going to get the sounds that we wanted," Allom said. To make up for that, the band wired rooms throughout the mansion, putting the drums in a stone hallway and guitars in separate rooms. They were also creative with sound effects on the record.[18]

"In those days we used to invent everything we could in weird and wonderful ways," Tipton said. "It was really good fun."[19]

They used the sounds of trays of silverware, pool sticks, smashed bottles, police sirens, and slamming doors.

"It's telling a story with sound," said Halford. "You're actually seeing a movie running through your head. That's one of the things that I've always loved to do as a lyricist. I love to write movies in your head. When you bring in those extra dimensions of sound like the smashing glass and the police sirens, it's just reinforcing what you're trying to say."[20]

The album features several Judas Priest classics. "Living After Midnight" is a catchy song about partying—one of the few songs on that subject the band ever wrote. "Breakin' the Law" told the story of a working-class person who is without a job and turns to a life of crime. "Metal Gods" was a song about robots, inspired by Halford's love of science fiction movies. The sound of the robots' marching feet was made in the studio by banging trays of silverware. But while the song has its roots in science fiction, many people thought of it as referring to the band itself.[21]

"As time went on I suppose we became metal gods to some people," Tipton said.[22]

British Steel has a sense of joy to it, with songs about having fun, not compromising, and staying true to yourself and united with like-minded others.

The album features a hand holding a razor blade on the cover. Halford said that was an accurate picture of what the album sounds like. "It almost has that kind of stainless steel quality about it. The songs just cut through. There's no messing around. They're direct and sharp and to the point," he said.[23]

The album was Judas Priest's first gold album in the United States, which means it sold more than five hundred thousand copies.

To promote *British Steel*, Judas Priest turned to filming music videos, which was a new art form at the time. They released videos for the singles "Living After Midnight" and "Breakin' the Law." An extensive world tour in support of *British Steel* included dates in the United States with opening acts Def Leppard and the Scorpions.[24]

Judas Priest traveled to the Spanish island of Ibiza to record the next album, *Point of Entry*. After the triumph of *British Steel*, many thought *Point of Entry* was a step in the wrong direction.

In an interview, Tipton explained that the album's title was a reflection of Judas Priest's new direction. "It means a lot of things to us," Tipton said. "We've just started the '80s and that's the main thing about it. We've always felt that we're a band that's changed with the times . . . never really sticking to a 1973 vein of sluggish riffs. And we just felt this title was very appropriate. It's slightly different from anything we've ever done, but it's still within the range of Judas Priest."[25]

The album was more commercial sounding and received mixed reactions from fans and critics alike. Years later, Tipton admitted that it wasn't entirely successful.

"There are good tracks on there," Tipton said. "There are tracks that aren't my personal favorites, like 'You Say Yes.' They're melodic and good, but they're not really Judas Priest songs as such. It was experimenting, and there's nothing wrong with that."[26]

But Hill said that *Point of Entry* reflected what the band wanted to do at that time.

"We didn't make a conscious effort where we went 'We'd better try and sell this to the teeny boppers.' There was none of that. It was just that we went in the studio and did what we did. There was no conscious effort to make it commercial, it just turned out the way that it did," said Hill.[27]

Judas Priest was featured on the cover of *CREEM* magazine in August 1981. The magazine held a contest to give away the 1979 Harley-Davidson motorcycle Halford used on stage for the previous year.

"Tipton and Downing are exceptional guitarists—tasteful, in fact, considering the decibels," wrote J. Kordosh in *CREEM*. "I doubt too many bands could even keep up with these guys onstage."[28]

Three music videos were released from *Point of Entry*—"Don't Go," "Heading Out to the Highway," and "Hot Rockin'."

Point of Entry wasn't the high point of Judas Priest's career. The album confused some fans, but on the tour that followed, Judas Priest saw bigger live audiences than ever before. The stage was set for Priest's biggest successes.

While many consider *British Steel* to be Priest's best album, 1982's *Screaming for Vengeance* is the one that brought the band commercial success, radio airplay, and turned them into international superstars.

For the sessions that created *Screaming for Vengeance*, Judas Priest returned to the island of Ibiza and also spent time in Florida. The band concentrated so hard on making the record, they worked right through a hurricane.[29]

It was the band's first double-platinum album in the United States (meaning sales of more than 2 million copies). "We were made for America and America fell in love with the band," said Tipton.[30]

The album was dark and paranoid, dealing with such themes as nuclear war and government cruelty. The cover featured a fierce-looking robotic bird called the Hellion. It began with the instrumental "The Hellion," which kicked right into "Electric Eye," a song about a future world where people were always being watched by some all-knowing authority figure. Those two songs provided a potent opening pair that Judas Priest often used to open its concerts.

But it was another song—the catchy but defiant "You've Got Another Thing Comin'"—that became Judas Priest's biggest radio hit.

"That song was very much an accident," explained Hill. He said the band was running short on time in the studio and needed another song to fill the record. "That is very unusual for us because we never take that sort of attitude," he said. "[I]t was written and recorded within hours. It was an after-thought. It might have been because it was so spontaneous and fresh that American radio picked up on it and the next thing you know it was being played all over the place. It was the song that broke us in a big way in the States. Everything that followed really owed itself to that song."[31]

Not only was *Screaming for Vengeance* a hit with fans, but critics liked it, too. *All Music Guide*'s Steve Huey described it as "a catchy, accessible metal record in the best sense of the description, and it rivals *British Steel* as Priest's best album of the '80s."[32]

Reviewer Joe Fernbacher compared Priest to some of the other metal bands of the time—including Black Sabbath. "After a listen to *Screaming for Vengeance*, all else pales, even those metal bands that ARE good like Def Leppard, Girlschool and Van Halen. This record is about as far ahead of its time as Black Sabbath's Sabotage was, still is and probably always will be," wrote Fernbacher.[33] Judas Priest went on its longest American tour to date from 1982 through 1983 in support of *Screaming for Vengeance*.[34]

That tour inspired two films. The first was a live video of one concert on the tour. The second, *Heavy Metal Parking Lot*, showed the band's dedicated fans before a concert.

The tour capped off with the band's proud performance at the US Festival in 1983. The band was bigger than ever, but life on the road wasn't always easy.

"Eventually life is all one big tour. Trying to divide them up into even years is really quite difficult," Downing said.[35]

The band was riding high, and the never-ending tour showed no signs of stopping yet.

DEFENDING THE FAITH

After the triumph of *Screaming for Vengeance*, Judas Priest was on top of the world. The band was reaping the benefits of being one of the most popular and most respected heavy metal bands on the planet. But they had no way of knowing that storm clouds were gathering on the horizon.

The band returned to Ibiza and Florida to record 1984's *Defenders of the Faith* album. While mixing the album in Miami, the band members also sat for interviews with journalist Steve Gett for an official biography that was released in 1984.

Defenders of the Faith built on the pattern created by *Screaming for Vengeance*. The cover features another fictional robot beast—this one called the Metallian. The Metallian looks something like a cross between a lion, a bear, and a tank. On the massive headlining tour in support of *Defenders of the Faith*, the band's stage show featured a giant silver Metallian, which would pick Halford up in its giant paw. With the songs "Freewheel Burning," "Rock Hard Ride Free," "Heavy Duty," and "Love Bites," the album was filled with strong heavy metal anthems.

"It pretty well summed up where we are," Halford said of the album. He explained:

JUDAS PRIEST IN THE 1980S. FROM LEFT TO RIGHT: DAVE HOLLAND, K.K. DOWNING, ROB HALFORD, GLENN TIPTON, AND IAN HILL.

If you take the analysis of what the title means, instantly Judas Priest are 'defending the faith,' the faith being heavy metal music. And we're defending it . . . from the people that knock it, and from it ever going out of style or fashion, which we never thought it would anyway. What's more, we figured that *Defenders of the Faith* was apt, not only for Priest, but for all heavy metal freaks around the world. The fans, the bands—it's a statement for everybody.[1]

In contrast to the band's early career, heavy metal was now riding high on a newfound wave of popularity. As one of heavy metal's most innovative bands, Judas Priest found itself competing with much younger bands—many of which looked to Priest for inspiration.

"We're perfectly aware of the fact that we're surrounded by other bands all trying to get to the top," Halford told *Circus* magazine. "But we can't let that worry us. The main pressure you feel going out on a tour like this is knowing that you've really got to put your whole self across to entertain, to impress and to let people see you're the best.[2]

In 1985, Judas Priest's only concert appearance was Live Aid, which was a massive charity concert held in London and Philadelphia to help starving people in Africa. Halford also participated in the heavy metal charity single Hear 'N' Aid.[3]

But 1985 also marked the year that Judas Priest—and heavy metal artists in general—began to receive criticism for lyrical content. A group called the Parents' Music Resource

Rob Halford with Judas Priest performed in the 1985 Live Aid concert.

Center (PMRC) was formed in Washington, D.C. Its members included Tipper Gore, the wife of then-senator (and future vice president) Al Gore, and Susan Baker, the wife of the treasury secretary, James Baker. Judas Priest's song "Eat Me Alive" from *Defenders of the Faith* was included on a list of objectionable songs created by the PMRC called the "Filthy 15."

The PMRC's protests led the recording industry to put parental advisory stickers on records that may have explicit lyrics. Encouraged by the PMRC, in September 1985, a U.S. Senate committee held hearings on whether references to sex, drugs, and violence should be regulated in rock lyrics. The committee considered including a rating system for records like there is for movies.[4]

"Parents have been yelling about rock-and-roll forever," said Susan Baker. "But they don't know that the lyrics have changed, and a line has been crossed."[5]

Some in the industry were afraid that a new law would mean that the government would be able to control what artists could say—a kind of control called censorship.

"This is absolutely a move toward censorship," said Danny Goldberg, president of Gold Mountain Records. "All of us worry most about freedom of speech when it affects our own outlet. Rating records would undermine the creative process and undermine the economic structure of the business. A lunatic fringe minority is trying to subvert one of the most wonderful aspects of our culture."[6]

Some people said it was important for parents to take responsibility for what their children listen to. Ira Glasser, the executive director of the American Civil Liberties Union, said in response to the proposal: "As a parent of teen-age children, I can protect them without the help of their rating system. They can control their own kids and leave mine alone."[7]

During the hearings, musicians Frank Zappa, John Denver, and heavy metal singer Dee Snider from the band Twisted Sister testified. No rating system was ever put in place, but the parental advisory labels are still used on albums today. And the PMRC were not the last people to criticize Judas Priest's music for its content.

Judas Priest's next album, *Turbo*, was released in 1986. It is one of the most controversial records of the band's career. It featured guitar synthesizers and a slick sound that was different from what fans had become accustomed to.

Talking about the digital effects, Halford said the band was determined to discover "the most advanced and sophisticated way of recording our music."[8] Despite the different sound, the singles "Turbo Lover" and "Locked In" were big hits for the band.

The sound wasn't the only thing that was changing. Even though Judas Priest created the metal look, by the time *Turbo* was released, the members decided it was time for something different. Halford grew out his hair, and the new costumes featured more color.

"In actual fact we are changing the image somewhat on this world tour," Halford said, "to drop all the studs and the chains and the whips . . ."[9] He continued:

> What we've done is take the strong parts of our image—
> the leather and the tough, aggressive look—and we've
> tried to make it a bit more *stylish*, if that's the right
> word. The way this album was developing, we went to
> our costume designer in L.A. and said: "Look, Ray, we
> feel it's time for a change. We don't want you to give us a
> *wimpy* look by any means, but can you take the essential
> ingredients of what we're about—the power and the
> strength—and incorporate this into a new look?" So he
> went away and thought about it for months and months,
> and we put together a whole new bunch of outfits. It's
> difficult to describe them actually, but I think it's a step
> in the right direction. The sound, the album cover and
> the look of the band is now very *1986*.[10]

In part, the band was inspired to change its look because so many other bands had adopted it.

"We want to look as modern and strong as the music," Halford said. "The leather look has become a bit dated. Other bands picked it up from us and we feel we've moved beyond that. It's essential to keep moving in every way possible."[11]

The band's busy schedule continued to be exhausting.

"Being in Priest is a tremendous amount of fun," Tipton

said, "but at the same time it involves a lot of hard work. If the band isn't busy in the studio, we're generally out on the road and so you get very little time to yourself. But that's OK; we're not complaining. It took us 10 years to get where we are today and, now that we've become successful on an international level, there's no way we can afford to take things easy."[12]

And they didn't take it easy. The *Turbo* tour featured the band's biggest stage show so far.[13]

The *Turbo* tour also spawned a live album called *Priest . . . Live* in 1987. It was recorded during concerts in Dallas and Atlanta. A full-length live video was also released at the time.

For 1988's *Ram It Down* album, Judas Priest returned to a harder sound after the experimental *Turbo*. During this time, a new style of heavy metal was gaining popularity. This type of music, known as "speed metal" or "thrash metal," was even louder, faster, and more outrageous than the music Priest was known for. Bands, such as Metallica, Anthrax, Megadeth, and Slayer were taking metal to a whole new level of power, and Priest responded.

Ram It Down was recorded during a frigid winter in Denmark, in contrast to previous records, which had been recorded in the warm climates of Spain and Florida. It proved to be the final album for both producer Tom Allom and drummer Dave Holland.[14]

Soon, the members of Judas Priest would have to defend

themselves in court over something a pair of troubled fans did several years earlier.

In December 1985, Judas Priest fans eighteen-year-old Raymond Belknap and twenty-year-old James Vance listened to the *Stained Class* record for six hours while smoking marijuana and drinking beer. The two young men took a shotgun to a playground at a church and shot themselves. Belknap died right away. Vance destroyed most of his face but lived for three more years.[15]

The parents and Belknap's estate sued Judas Priest, arguing that Vance and Belknap had become mesmerized, or obsessed by the music, and that's what caused the pair to shoot themselves.[16]

The suit claimed that the band recorded hidden messages—also known as subliminal messages—onto the album, and that those messages convinced the two youths to form a suicide pact. The band and its label, CBS, were accused of producing a faulty product, as well as negligence and intentional and reckless misconduct.[17]

Judas Priest's manager denied that there were subliminal messages on the record, and he wondered why anybody would think a band would do such a thing.

"I don't know what subliminals are, but I do know there's nothing like that in this music," said Judas Priest's manager Bill Curbishley. "If we were going to do that, I'd be saying,

'Buy seven copies,' not telling a couple of screwed-up kids to kill themselves."[18]

Halford agreed with Curbishley, saying: "Why on earth would any band want to go and kill its fans? Because these boys were hardcore Judas Priest fans. They came from a very tough family life. There was a history of alcohol abuse, there was a history of drug abuse, and the boys were finding solace in the music of Judas Priest."[19]

But instead of blaming drug use or rough family life for the youths' suicides, the lawyer representing the Belknap family blamed Judas Priest. He said the fact that Judas Priest appealed to troubled people made the band more responsible.

"The members of the chess club, the math and science majors don't listen to this stuff. It's the dropouts, the drug and alcohol abusers," said Kenneth McKenna, the lawyer for Belknap's family. "So our argument is you have a duty to be more cautious when you're dealing with a population suscep-tible to this stuff."[20]

In August 1988, the Nevada Supreme Court refused to dismiss the lawsuit, which meant the band had to stand trial in Reno.[21]

Many commentators came to Judas Priest's defense. Jon Pareles of the *New York Times* wrote that "rock gets singled out because it reaches teen-agers and seems to exclude par-ents—it's a great, noisy unknown."[22] He continued:

Entertainment and art that address frightening events and extreme emotions are probably as old as art itself. And rock that tells teen-agers that they face a dangerous, irrational, brutal world tells them the unsanitized truth. It also tells each worried teen-ager that others have been terrified and enraged, and that they can expect more emotional turbulence than they'll ever see on sitcoms or in movies of the week. It's not the job of any performer to be a babysitter or peer counselor or a role model, but speed-metal bands strike a chord with millions of teen-agers because they reflect what's on their minds—and the songs tell them they are not alone.[23]

For the band, the lawsuit was devastating. "We were very upset. We thought that the allegations were completely ridiculous and without foundation. But the only way we could put our side of the story across and to tell everybody the truth was to go to Reno and sit in a courthouse for five weeks and deal with each issue as it was presented to us. That was a very upsetting time for us to go through," Halford said.[24]

The trial began in July 1990. Halford testified on August 1, 1990, giving the court a ten-second a cappella (without accompaniment) demonstration of his singing style.[25]

After seventeen days and forty witnesses, the band was cleared on August 25. Judge Jerry Whitehead said that the plaintiffs lost the case because they didn't prove the band intentionally put hidden messages on the album that caused the two young men to kill themselves.[26]

"We've come out without a blemish, and we're absolutely thrilled and delighted," said Halford after he received the news.[27]

In the wake of the trial, Judas Priest released *Painkiller* in 1990. It was the band's first album with former Racer X drummer Scott Travis, who replaced Dave Holland in the band. The album was recorded in France with producer Chris Tsangarides, who also worked on *Sad Wings of Destiny*.[28] The album was well-received and was nominated for a Grammy Award for best metal performance.

New York Times writer Jon Pareles described how the band's fans found refuge in Priest music:

> Often, the lyrics agonize about falling under the control of outside forces, mirroring teen-agers' worries about impending adult choices, while battering-ram guitar chords and pounding drumbeats invoke both ominous power and, through enjoyment of the noise, the chance to hold out against that power. Judas Priest's fans shouted along with bad-news choruses as if they offered release.[29]

Judas Priest toured with Alice Cooper and Motorhead in the spring of 1991. The tour ended at the C.N.E. Gardens in Toronto, which turned out to be the last Priest show for nearly seven years.[30]

Between the constant recording and touring and the stress of the Reno trial, Halford was ready for a break from Priest.

"At the end of the *Painkiller* tour, I think there was just a feeling of absolute physical and mental exhaustion," Halford said. "We were in agreement that I was going to step out and do some work with other players, but it was only when we got into the horrific end of legal contracts and everything that things began to get really difficult."[31]

Halford officially left the band in 1992. The split quickly became nasty, sparking a longstanding and messy public battle between Halford and his former bandmates.

"Almost inevitably, a bitter feud arose between both parties that grew stronger over the next few years, with issued statements being batted back and forth between lawyers," wrote Neil Daniels.[32]

Halford launched a new band called Fight, which also featured drummer Scott Travis. The band released its first album, *War of Words*, in 1993. For the singer, it marked the beginning of a period of creativity. For the first time, he was writing and producing all of the music. He released two more albums with Fight—1994's *Mutations* and 1995's *A Small Deadly Space*.

"I felt re-energized, and I just welcomed it, although I was tinged with sadness by being away from the band I loved the most," Halford said.[33]

New York Times reviewer Jon Pareles described Fight as "vigorous and efficient."[34] He wrote:

> Like the final versions of Judas Priest, Fight plays stomping metal, at slow and fast tempos, to carry Mr. Halford's long-suffering words. . . . As with Judas Priest, Mr. Halford tosses together private resentment, fears of apocalypse and glimmers of blasphemy. He sings in a falsetto shriek, a baritone croon or a growl, allotting one vocal style per song, with a mannered vibrato that a 14-year-old might find spooky.[35]

After Halford left the band, the other members of Judas Priest were left without a direction. The band released a best-of collection called *Metalworks* in 1993, and Tipton started pursuing a solo career in 1994.

Tipton said, "There was no Judas Priest as such, and it didn't look as though there was going to be." He entered the studio in 1995 to pursue a solo career.[36]

"The future looked bleak," Tipton said. "I decided I couldn't just crawl in the corner and die, so I started putting pen to paper and wrote some songs. I had no idea what for or who I was going to work with."[37]

For the first time in his career, Tipton sang lead on the album.

"My vocal ability is very limited, but I'm fortunate in that I can write the songs around my vocal limitations," Tipton said. "I've got the luxury to tailor make the songs so I can sing them."[38]

The original sessions for the album featured famous session drummer Cozy Powell and John Entwistle, who was the legendary bassist for The Who. "The label liked the material but suggested that the lineup was a little 'old school' and that I should work with some younger musicians and blend the new tracks in to give the album a more modern feel," Tipton wrote. "This I did as I had very little choice at the time and in all honesty a very good album emerged."[39]

In 1997, Atlantic Records released Tipton's first album, *Baptizm of Fire*. Powell was killed in a car crash in 1998, and Entwistle died of a cocaine-related heart attack in 2002. In a tribute to Tipton's collaborators, the original sessions were eventually released in 2006 on an album called *Edge of the World*.

In January 1995, Judas Priest announced that it was looking for a new singer.[40] Over the next year, the band received more than a thousand tapes from singers who wanted to join the band.[41]

In October 1997, Judas Priest announced that Halford was being replaced by a new singer named Tim Owens from Akron, Ohio. Even though the band hadn't played a concert since 1991, Downing was confident that the band would be able to reclaim its title as one of the greatest metal bands in the world.

Owens had something of a Cinderella story. He was a big fan of Judas Priest from the time he was a youngster.

"His room—walls and ceiling—was nothing but posters of Judas Priest," Owens' mother Sherri told the *New York Times*.[42]

Owens was the singer for a band called Winters Bane. He worked selling office products by day and sang by night. Winters Bane released an album in 1994, but the band had more success working as a Judas Priest tribute band called British Steel. Owens would book Winters Bane to open British Steel shows.[43]

"It worked great," Owens told the *New York Times*. "We went from getting $50 a show to $1,000. I'd sing 45 minutes of Winters Bane originals, then put on leather and do two hours of Priest. People would look up and say 'Hey, isn't that the same guy?'"[44]

The band found out about Owens after a homemade videotape of one of his 1995 performances was given to Priest drummer Scott Travis—without Owens' knowledge. The band watched it and could hardly believe what they were hearing. The band members thought he was lip-synching to Halford's original vocals.

"He sounded so much like Rob in certain registers you'd be stupid to think it was real," Downing said.[45]

The band contacted Owens and flew him to England to audition. He sang the first verse of "Victim of Changes" and was offered the job.[46]

Judas Priest returned to the studio with Owens to record 1997's *Jugulator* and 1998's live album *Meltdown*. The song "Bullet Train" from *Jugulator* was nominated for a Grammy Award for best metal performance.

"I've got so many [memories] really but I think that, probably, being nominated for a Grammy in America and going to the Grammys was the best," Owens said. "It was an amazing time."[47]

In 1997, Tim "Ripper" Owens (center) became the new lead singer for Judas Priest.

Halford kept busy. He formed a new electronic industrial-style group called Two, which signed to Interscope records in 1997, releasing the album *Voyeurs* in 1998. But the biggest news was that, by 1998, Halford was ready to tell the world about his homosexuality. He made the statement on *MTV News*.

"I think that most people know that I've been a gay man all of my life, and it's only been in recent times that it's an issue that I feel comfortable to address, and an issue that has been with me ever since recognizing my own sexuality," Halford said.[48]

Halford told *MTV News* that his sexuality was "something that I've been comfortable with forever," but he added that some people had problems with his homosexuality, which is called homophobia.

"A lot of homophobia still exists in the music world, in all kinds of music," Halford said. "I wouldn't say it's any more phobic in metal or rap or whatever this music is that I'm doing now, but that's just something I think we all have to address in our own lives. If we have a problem with it, I think we should seek help and find out why do we have a problem with it."[49]

Halford said he hoped his disclosure would help other people—particularly teenagers.

"I think it's difficult for everybody . . . in making the decision to come forward and be who you are, based on peer pressure, especially if you're a teenager," Halford said. "That's where a lot of the anxiety begins, and so maybe people like myself and others that do step in front of a camera and let the world know, maybe it's of some help, where there's an individual that's been successful, that's been able to achieve dreams and visions and goals in life and not let the issue of sexuality be something to hold them back, so I think it's an important thing."[50]

His former bandmates—who knew of Halford's homosexuality all along—responded to the news on MTV as well. Downing let out a mock yawn, and Hill responded, "It must have been the worst kept secret in rock and roll."[51]

Many were surprised at how well the news was received in the metal community—but not Halford.

"I think it destroys the myth of the so-called intolerance and homophobia that was supposedly existing in heavy metal," Halford said.[52]

Telling the world that he is a gay man was a positive experience for Halford.

"I wanted to do it for myself, like any gay man or lesbian woman," he said. "I was always protective of Judas Priest. I always felt that had I done this any earlier, or had I done it under different circumstances, the fallout would have damaged the band. And I would never do anything to hurt the band or its reputation or its following."[53]

In 2004, Judas Priest was a part of Ozzfest. From left to right: Rob Halford, Glenn Tipton, and Ian Hill.

JUDAS RISING

6

With the dawn of 2000, Judas Priest was still broken into two camps. The Ripper Owens-led Judas Priest continued to record and tour. Rob Halford had been criticized by some for his work with Two and returned to his roots with a new band called Halford.

In 2000, Halford (the band) released its first album, *Resurrection*. The band featured guitarists Metal Mike Chlasciak and Roy Z., bassist Mike Davis, and drummer Bobby Jarzombek. *Resurrection* was followed by 2001's *Live Insurrection* and 2002's *Crucible*.

In 2001, Judas Priest released a new studio album called *Demolition*. It was the band's first new album since 1997's *Jugulator*.

Tipton produced the album, and he said he tried to find a balance between a classic metal sound and a more modern edge:

> It has got tracks that are poised between old and new, so there is quite a bit of diversity on there, but I think that when all is said and done and if you view *Demolition* as a whole, it is classic Priest, but classic Priest evolved a bit. It is difficult to get it right and you can't please everybody and there will always be a percentage of fans, though they may be big Priest fans, who will feel the need to criticize us. After thirty years I can take a bit of criticism as long as it is constructive, but I do have to tell you, when we get it right it is gratifying *really*.[1]

Owens said, "I think this album's got that 'Jugulator' edge at times but it goes beyond once again. It actually goes back towards the classic Priest sounds at times."[2]

Demolition earned some good reviews. *Rolling Stone* writer Arion Berger wrote that the album "has a clean and direct sound, all red meat and bare arms, sinister choruses, chugging pace and those hysterical lake-of-fire vocal harmonies emblematic of vintage metal."[3]

Owens' story of moving from Priest fan to band member inspired a Hollywood movie starring Mark Wahlberg and Jennifer Aniston called *Rock Star*.

Even though the film was loosely based on Owens, the band took issue with some of the ways the movie differed from the true story.

"We have nothing to do with it," Owens said, adding that the real story would make a better movie because "it's a very interesting story about a normal person—not the rock & roll clichés of sex, drugs, rock & roll." He added, "It's unfortunate they have to make it Hollywood though, because what's better than having a guy who lives in the same town he grew up in and has the same friends and actually gets married?"[4]

Music channel VH1 filmed an episode of its *Behind The Music* series about Judas Priest in 2001. The episode gives the history of the band from its earliest days. It ends with Halford re-establishing contact with his bandmates in 2000 and inviting them to his parents' fiftieth wedding anniversary party. Downing and Hill attended the party, marking the first time they had seen Halford in nearly a decade.

"I do miss the band a lot," Halford said. "I miss the music. I miss all the great times we had together. But on top of those feelings, I feel more satisfied and complete now. One day it will all make sense."[5]

The newfound connection between the old bandmates had many people wondering if the classic Judas Priest lineup would reunite. Owens said that people were telling him that Halford wanted to be back in the band. He was prepared for that to happen, but he said he didn't think it would.

"It wouldn't upset me. It's business you know and I wouldn't burn any bridges. I would move on, be friends with the band and hopefully still work with the band. I don't know if they could ever work with Rob. Maybe a tour, maybe a show but I don't think they can work with him anymore," Owens said.[6]

A live album and accompanying DVD titled *Live in London* was released in 2003. Recorded live at the Brixton Academy in 2001, *Live in London* featured a set list that included "The Sentinel" and "Beyond the Realms of Death."

Judas Priest soldiered on with Owens at the mic, but not all was well. Neither *Jugulator* nor *Demolition* sold as well as the band's biggest records, and the band's following wasn't as big as it once had been. Soon, Judas Priest turned to its former lead singer to try and turn things around.

Even though it took several years, the seeds for a reunion were sown when Halford sent a letter to Tipton, Downing, and Hill back in 1999.

"I wrote an extensive letter just telling them how I felt. I think that was part of the very slow rebuilding process. I think you just go to the music, because somehow it's bigger than everybody," Halford said.[7]

Halford met with his former bandmates in July 2003 to discuss an upcoming box set chronicling the band's career. It was during that meeting that the idea of reuniting came up.

"I think the emotions of that box set, looking at all of the incredible things that we'd done together musically just came to the top," Halford said. "The final question at the end of that meeting 'Well, are we going to reunite? Are we even going to consider reuniting?' and we just looked each other in the eye and said 'We've got to go for it.'"[8]

Because the split with Halford was very public, very messy, and created some legal battles, there were some issues that needed to be addressed before any reunion could take place.

"We had to work on our friendship," Tipton said, "but all the bridges have been rebuilt and we put that animosity behind us."[9]

Ultimately, the strong bond between the band members helped them overcome their differences.

"It was very emotional," Tipton said. "When I saw Rob, we decided right then to reunite and go back out there. It felt just like it did before he left the band. And the world's gone just mad about it. It's very exciting."[10]

When the band announced that Halford was coming back to the band, the metal world was thrilled. Halford said that showed "the great love and power of the music of Judas Priest."[11]

"This has been wanted and pleaded for for so many years. And obviously, with us all being in our separate worlds musically, we haven't really been able to seriously consider it until now," Halford said.[12]

"It's been almost a five-year process of rebuilding our friendship and musical bridges," Halford added. "So, this reunion has taken a lot of love and repair work and obviously we're thrilled that it's finally happened now."[13]

But with Halford's return, Owens found himself out of a job. After being dismissed from Priest, though, he landed on his feet. He had already recorded the vocals for an album by the band Iced Earth when the news came that Halford was rejoining Judas Priest. He joined Iced Earth as a permanent member and remained grateful for his time in Judas Priest.

"I'm here today because of Judas Priest," he told *Rolling Stone*. "Yeah, I'm a talented singer, but luck is involved when Judas Priest gives you a call."[14]

The reunion news was received with much excitement in the heavy metal world. The reunited Judas Priest joined the 2004 Ozzfest tour, co-headlining with fellow Birmingham natives and metal legends Black Sabbath.

The Halford-led version of Judas Priest hadn't played live in thirteen years, and many people wondered what they would sound like. The show earned positive reviews, including in the *New York Times*. The band "played an immaculate set, all old hits, with all the old falsetto screams rendered accurately," wrote Ben Ratliff of the *New York Times*. "This was the only set with costume changes and stage props: the singer had a succession of cloaks, studded and leather and velvet. In 'Hell

Bent for Leather,' he re-enacted his trademark gesture of riding to center stage on a motorcycle."[15]

A reviewer named Soft Boy wrote on the *Metal Express Radio* Web site that Judas Priest "seemed like a family again, happy to be in each other's company on stage and benefiting from a profound trust and loyalty towards one another." He added, "Overall and to the satisfaction of the audience, this show was possibly the 'best' JP has sounded during their storied career."[16]

For Halford, it felt good to be back with his band—and to be able to be open about his sexuality.

"Metal audiences today are capable of accepting all kinds of sexualities as much as colors of your skin or religious beliefs," Halford told *VH1.com*. "So I've just been thrilled to be so openly greeted and welcomed home. It's been an experience of pure pleasure with not one moment of rejection or hate."[17]

The career-spanning box set that led to the band's reunion, called *Metalogy*, was released in 2004. The box set featured four CDs containing sixty-five songs. The box was covered in black leather and silver studs. It included the band's hits, live songs, unreleased demos, and other rare songs. The first edition of the box also featured a DVD of a complete concert recorded on the *Screaming for Vengeance* tour.

"It's a testament to the power of Priest's music that from generation to generation people are still intrigued by the band," Halford told *Rolling Stone*. "The interest never dies. It's there for albums that are twenty-five years old and it's there for the next one. It's great to have this history, but still be able to debunk the dinosaur thing."[18]

But even as Judas Priest revisited its past glories, Halford insisted the band wasn't going to become merely a nostalgia act.

"I just feel very secure and strong in the knowledge that the band is going to forge ahead and continue to be a significant and vital force," Halford told *Rolling Stone*. "All these years later, Priest is still in demand. And I think it's not just about seeing the original lineup on stage, it's also about 'Well, what are they going to do next?' The storm has already begun."[19]

The band began writing for a new album with Halford. Even though they hadn't written songs together since *Painkiller*, the process was familiar and comfortable.

"From the first day of writing, it was very spontaneous," Halford said. "It was like returning to when we were kids and we had no problems or difficulties in just letting the metal roar out."[20]

Tipton agreed that it was good to rekindle the writing relationship with Halford.

"We've got a writing formula with Rob that works, and we're very lucky we've got that," Tipton said. "We get riffs and musical ideas and structures and we all meet up with Rob, who has lyrical ideas and we kick the ideas around until the room lights up. Then we start again with another idea."[21]

The new record, *Angel of Retribution*, had Judas Priest returning to top form.

"It's got a little bit of everything," Halford said. "It's like some of the greatest moments of our career have suddenly come together on these songs. But that wasn't out of any attempt. It's just that the essence of the speed and thrust of these tracks are part of the stamp and tradition and heritage of Priest."[22]

Fans and critics alike were pleased with the way *Angel of Retribution* turned out. *Kerrang!* reviewer Dom Lawson wrote:

> Priest didn't invent heavy metal, but they certainly
> perfected the formula over numerous classic albums,
> providing the genre with its rulebook, rudiments and
> beloved clichés. And here they all are again, sounding
> fresher than ever. This is an album designed both to
> delight the faithful and to introduce metal's latest
> converts to the timeless sound of a seminal band on
> top form. Great songs, great riffs, controlled aggression,
> dazzling musicianship: this album simply bulges with
> all those things and more.[23]

With the reunion in full swing, Halford seemed at home. "I went through all these different seekings, and really looked to see if there was anything else that was calling me that would fulfill me as much as Judas Priest," Halford said. "And quite frankly, there's not. Not on this scale. I'm back where I belong."[24]

In 2006, Judas Priest announced that it was going to record a concept album about the French writer Nostradamus who wrote prophecies that some claim predicted historical events, such as the rise of Napoleon and Hitler and the September 11, 2001 terrorist attacks. The opera would address twenty key moments in Nostradamus' life.

Nostradamus practiced astrology, which is a belief that the positions of the moon, the sun, and the stars have an effect on human events, and that people can tell the future by studying the stars. People often refer to him as a prophet, which means he is a person who predicts the future.

He was born Michel de Nostredame in France in 1503. At a young age he showed signs of being bright and was educated in math, Latin, Greek, Hebrew, and astrology.[25] He became a doctor in 1525, during an outbreak of the plague in southern France. He became successful, but then his wife and children all died of disease and he wandered Europe.[26] He died in 1566.[27]

Halford said Nostradamus is the perfect subject for a heavy metal band to take up. "Nostradamus is all about metal, isn't he?" Halford told *MTV News*. "He had an amazing life that was full of trial and tribulation and joy and sorrow. He's a very human character and a world-famous individual. You can take his name and translate it into any language and

Gene Simmons of KISS (left) and Rob Halford after the VH1 Rock Honors concert in 2006

everybody knows about him, and that's important because we're dealing with a worldwide audience."[28]

Halford added that the subject of Nostradamus fit in with much of Priest's earlier work. "If you know anything about Priest, you know that we've made the characters come to life in songs like 'Painkiller,' 'The Sentinel' and 'The Sinner,' and now we're just taking that storytelling side of Priest that people love and cherish and putting all into a single project so it all comes to life in one dimension."[29]

In some ways, the challenges that Nostradamus faced in his life are like the challenges metal fans face. Halford said:

> Nostradamus obviously was a real human being. He
> went through a lot of trauma and a lot of incredible
> adventures. The research that I've done on him—coming
> as he did from the 16th century, dabbling in what was
> viewed by some people as the black arts, then being has-
> sled by the Catholic Church and other organizations—
> I can assimilate that into some aspects of the metal
> world, the way that we've always fought back at society
> and the rejection that we used to receive and to some
> extent might still get today. So it's all cool, isn't it?[30]

Judas Priest's influence on the world of heavy metal is undeniable. In 2006, VH1 paid tribute to that influence by including the band in its first annual *Rock Honors* show. Priest was honored along with KISS, Queen, and Def Leppard. Judas Priest performed "Breakin' the Law," "The Green Manalishi (With the Two-Pronged Crown)," and "You've Got

Another Thing Comin'" on the show, and the band Godsmack played "Electric Eye," "Victim of Changes," and "Hell Bent for Leather."

Nostradamus was released in 2008. The two-CD concept album saw the band again pushing the boundaries of heavy metal.

JUDAS PRIEST PERFORMS DURING THE ROCK HONORS CONCERT IN 2006. FROM LEFT TO RIGHT: ROB HALFORD, K.K. DOWNING, GLENN TIPTON, AND IAN HILL. SCOTT TRAVIS IS PLAYING THE DRUMS.

"For me, *Nostradamus* has been a musical journey without comparison," Downing said. "The intrigue and mystery that surrounds this revered man has expanded my perception of heavy metal to the highest plateau and enabled me to reach the outer limits of my imagination and transport unique feelings and emotions to the instrument that allows me to express myself."[31]

The band supported the release with a tour featuring the band Heaven and Hell, which is made up of members of Black Sabbath with singer Ronnie James Dio. Also on the tour was Motorhead and Testament.

Nobody knows what the future holds for Judas Priest, but it doesn't take a prophet like Nostradamus to imagine that no matter what happens, the band will continue to fly the heavy metal flag.

"We've always maintained we're a heavy metal band. Even during the time periods when metal was supposed to be unfashionable and other bands were trying to get rid of the term, we were proud to be heavy metal," said Tipton.[32]

And, for Halford, it remains a challenge of metal versus the world.

"By definition it should still be fighting against society. It should still be rattling cages, it should still be an irritant," Halford said. "And so you kick back. You kick back, you punch back, you fight back, you claw back, you scream back with heavy metal."[33]

TIMELINE

1970—Ian Hill and K.K. Downing form a band.

1971—Singer Al Atkins joins Hill and Downing's band. He brings the name Judas Priest from a previous band.

1973—Singer Rob Halford replaces Atkins in Judas Priest.

1974—Judas Priest signs to Gull Records; Glenn Tipton joins Judas Priest; First album *Rocka Rolla* is released.

1975—Judas Priest makes its television debut on *The Old Grey Whistle Test*.

1977—Judas Priest goes on its first American tour.

1979—The band's Japanese tour is documented on the live *Unleashed in the East* album.

1980—*British Steel* is released, becoming the band's first gold record in the United States.

1982—The single "You've Got Another Thing Comin'" becomes a radio hit.

1983—Judas Priest plays the US Festival, helping usher in a new wave of heavy metal popularity.

1985—Judas Priest plays the Live Aid charity concert; The Parents' Music Resource Center adds the Judas Priest song "Eat Me Alive" to its "Filthy 15" list of objectionable songs.

1988—*Ram It Down* is released.

1989—Drummer Dave Holland is replaced by Scott Travis.

1990—Judas Priest stands trial in a civil case relating to the suicides of two young fans. After a five-week trial, the band is cleared of the accusations.

1991—Rob Halford plays his last show with Judas Priest before leaving the band.

1992—Rob Halford officially quits Judas Priest for a solo career with his new band, Fight.

1997—Glenn Tipton releases the solo album *Baptizm of Fire;* Tim "Ripper" Owens is selected as Judas Priest's new singer and the band releases *Jugulator* with him at the mic.

1998—Rob Halford reveals that he is a gay man.

1999—Rob Halford sends a letter to his former bandmates in Judas Priest hoping to mend fences.

2000—Rob Halford forms a new band, called Halford, and releases *Resurrection*; K.K. Downing and Ian Hill attend the fiftieth wedding anniversary party of Rob Halford's parents.

2001—VH1 makes an episode of its *Behind The Music* series about Judas Priest.

2003—Rob Halford rejoins Judas Priest.

2004—The career-spanning retrospective box set *Metalogy* is released.

2005—*Angel of Retribution*, the first studio album with Rob Halford since 1990, is released.

2006—VH1 pays tribute to Judas Priest in the first annual *Rock Honors* awards show.

2008—*Nostradamus* is released; Judas Priest goes on tour.

DISCOGRAPHY

Rocka Rolla (1974)

Sad Wings of Destiny (1976)

Sin After Sin (1977)

Stained Class (1978)

Hell Bent for Leather (1979)

Unleashed in the East (1979)

British Steel (1980)

Point of Entry (1981)

Screaming for Vengeance (1982)

Defenders of the Faith (1984)

Turbo (1986)

Priest . . . Live (1986)

Ram It Down (1988)

Painkiller (1990)

Metal Works '73–'93 (1993)

Jugulator (1997)

Meltdown (1998)

Demolition (2001)

Live in London (2003)

Metalogy (2004)

Angel of Retribution (2005)

Essential Judas Priest (2006)

Nostradamus (2008)

DVDs

Classic Albums-Judas Priest: British Steel (2001)

Judas Priest: Live in London (2001)

Electric Eye (2003)

Judas Priest: Rising in the East (2005)

Judas Priest: Live Vengeance '82 (2006)

CONCERT TOURS[1]

1974: Rocka Rolla Tour

1975–1976: Sad Wings of Destiny Tour

1977: Sin After Sin tour

1978: Stained Class Tour

1978–1979: Killing Machine/Hell Bent for Leather Tour

1980: British Steel Tour

1981: World Wide Blitz Tour

1982–1983: World Vengeance Tour

1984: Metal Conquerors/Defenders Tour

1986: Fuel For Life Tour

1988: Mercenaries of Metal Tour

1990–1991: Painkiller Tour

1998: Jugulator Tour

2001–2002: Demolition World Tour

2004: United Tour, Ozzfest

2005: Retribution Tour

2008: Masters of Metal Tour

GLOSSARY

censorship—When freedom of expression is curtailed by a group in authority.

genre—A style of music. Heavy metal, country, and hip-hop are all genres of music.

headbanger—A fan of heavy metal music. The term comes from the way some heavy metal fans thrash their heads up and down.

heavy metal—A style of music that features loud guitars, soaring vocals, and pounding drums. Judas Priest is considered one of the originators of heavy metal.

hellion—A rowdy person. Also the name of the fictitious robotic bird on the cover of *Screaming for Vengeance*.

homophobia—The fear of homosexuality.

homosexual—A person who is sexually attracted to others of the same sex. Gay is another term for homosexual.

LP—A full-length album, from the term "long player."

plaintiff—A person who files a lawsuit.

riff—A repeated musical phrase. Heavy metal music is known for its distinctive riffs.

subliminal messages—Hidden messages that some believe can influence a person without that person knowing.

CHAPTER NOTES

Chapter 1. Heavy Metal Sunday

1. Tommy Lee, Mick Mars, Vince Neil, Nikki Sixx, and Neil Strauss, *The Dirt* (New York: ReaganBooks, 2002), p. 90.

2. *Heavy: The Story of Metal*, VH1 documentary, 2006.

3. Rob Kemp, "Judas Priest: *Metalogy*," record review, *Rolling Stone*, May 17, 2004, <http://www. rollingstone.com/news/story/6053626/new_cds_ morrissey_alanis> (December 3, 2007).

4. *Heavy: The Story of Metal.*

5. Nathan Brackett and Christian Hoard, *The New Rolling Stone Album Guide*, 4th edition (New York: Fireside, 2004), p. 444.

6. Andrew Dansby, "Judas Priest Forge New Steel," *Rolling Stone*, July 23, 2003, <http://www. rollingstone.com/news/story/5936738/judas_priest_ forge_new_steel> (December 5, 2007).

7. Geoff Barton, *Essential Judas Priest* CD liner notes.

8. Sylvie Simmons, "Judas Priest, Leathered, Studded Dudes Or . . ." *CREEM*, September 1986, *Rock's Backpages*, <http://www.rocksbackpages.com/ print.html?ArticleID=6865> (November 28, 2006).

Chapter 2. Who Is Judas Priest?

1. Rob Halford, *Fresh Air* radio interview, June 21, 2005, *NPR: National Public Radio*, <http://www.npr.org/templates/story/story.php?storyId=4712606> (December 5, 2007).

2. Ibid.

3. *Behind the Music: Judas Priest*, VH1 television, 2001.

4. Ibid.

5. Judy Wieder, "Judas Priest's Rob Halford Is First Heavy Metal Band Member to Say He Is Gay," *The Advocate*, May 12, 1998, *FindArticles.com*, <http://findarticles.com/p/articles/mi_m1589/is_n759/ai_20830600> (December 6, 2007).

6. *Behind the Music: Judas Priest*, VH1 television, 2001.

7. "K.K. Downing Biography," *K.K. Downing's Steel Mill*, n.d., <http://www.kkdowning.net/Bio/Bio.htm> (November 30, 2007).

8. "The Twin-Axe Attack: K.K. Downing and Glenn Tipton," *Judas Priest Info Pages*, n.d., <http://members.firstinter.net/markster/PROFILE2.html> (November 30, 2007).

9. Neil Daniels, *Judas Priest: Defenders of the Faith* (London: Omnibus Press, 2007), p. 26.

10. Garry Sharpe-Young, "Call for the Priest. K.K. Downing Opens up on Some of the Lesser Known Passages in the Band History," *Rockdetector*, March 3,

2006, <http://www.rockdetector.com/interviews/
artist, 33344.sm?id=80> (December 3, 2007).

11. Marco "Reddevil" Schmellentin, "K.K. Downing
In Depth Guitar Interview," *K.K. Downing's Steel
Mill*, March 2007, <http://www.kkdowning.net/
interviews/KKInGuitarDepth.htm> (November 30,
2007).

12. Jeff Kerby, "Exclusive: Judas Priest's Glenn
Tipton Still Ripping it Up," *KNAC.com*, September 10,
2002, <http://www.knac.com/article.asp?ArticleID
=1344> (November 30, 2007).

13. Michael Johansson, "Glenn Tipton Interview,"
Atlantis Online, 1986, <http://hem.bredband.net/
b136339/tipton.htm> (December 3, 2007).

14. David Wigg, "Glenn Tipton Interview,"
Chatshow.net, August 13, 2001, <http://www.chatshow.
net/interviews/interview.aspx?celebID=20&site=music>
(July 30, 2007).

15. Kerby.

16. "The Twin-Axe Attack: K.K. Downing and
Glenn Tipton."

17. Kerby.

18. Jeb Wright, "*Classic Rock Revisited* Presents
an Exclusive Interview With Judas Priest Bass
Player Ian Hill," *Classic Rock Revisited*, 1999,
<http://www.classicrockrevisited.com/ interviews99/
Ianhill.htm> (July 5, 2007).

19. ——, "Ian Hill of Judas Priest," *Classic Rock
Revisited*, 2002, <http://www.classicrockrevisited.com/

interviews02/ian_hill_interview_2002.htm> (July 30, 2007).

20. "The Sentinel: Ian Hill," *Judas Priest Info Pages*, n.d., <http://members.firstinter.net/markster/PROFILE3.html> (November 30, 2007).

21. Andrew C. Revkin, "A Metal-Head Becomes a Metal-God. Heavy," *The New York Times*, July 27, 1997, <http://query.nytimes.com/gst/fullpage.html?res=9901E0D8133BF 934A15754C0A961958260> (December 5, 2007).

22. Ibid.

23. "The Alumni: Les Binks, Dave Holland, and Ripper Owens," *Judas Priest Info Pages*, n.d., <http://members.firstinter.net/ markster/PROFILE5.html> (November 30, 2007).

24. Daniela P, "Face to Face With 'God,'" February 2, 1991, <http://user.tninet.se/~cxq849j/RobHal.html> (December 3, 2007).

25. "Drummer Guilty of Sex Attacks," *BBC News*, January 23, 2004,<http://news.bbc.co.uk/1/hi/england/northamptonshire/3423807.stm> (November 30, 2007).

26. "Ex-drummer Jailed for Sex Attacks," *BBC News*, February 13, 2004, <http://news.bbc.co.uk/1/hi/england/northamptonshire/3487095.stm> (November 30, 2007).

27. "The Machine Man: Scott Travis," *Judas Priest Info Pages*, n.d., <http://members.firstinter.net/ markster/PROFILE4.html> (November 30, 2007).

28. Paul Lefkowitz, "Drums.com Interview With Scott Travis," *Drums.Com*, 2000, <http://www.drums. com/interviews/scott.html> (December 3, 2007).

29. Ibid.

30. Daniela P.

Chapter 3. British Steel

1. Patricia S. Daniels and Stephen G. Hylsop, *Almanac of World History* (Washington, D.C.: National Geographic, 2006), p. 238.

2. Sean Lang, *British History for Dummies*, 2nd edition (Chichester, West Sussex, England: John Wiley & Sons Ltd., 2006), p. 259.

3. Daniels and Hyslop, p. 238.

4. Ibid., pp. 238–239.

5. Lang, p. 260.

6. Ibid.

7. Ibid., p. 347.

8. *Heavy: The Story of Metal*, VH1 documentary, 2006.

9. Ibid.

10. *Metal: A Headbanger's Journey*, Les Films Seville Pictures, 2005.

11. Ibid.

12. Jeb Wright, "Ian Hill of Judas Priest," *Classic Rock Revisited*, 2002, <http://www.classicrockrevisited.com/interviews02/ian_hill_interview_2002.htm> (July 30, 2007).

13. *Heavy: The Story of Metal.*

14. Ibid.

15. Ibid.

16. Sylvie Simmons, "Judas Priest, Leathered, Studded Dudes Or . . ." *CREEM*, September 1986, *Rock's Backpages*, <http://www.rocksbackpages.com/print.html?ArticleID=6865> (November 28, 2006).

17. Ibid.

18. Steve Gett, *Heavy Duty* (Port Chester, N.Y.: Cherry Lane Books, 1984), p. 23.

19. Ibid.

20. Krusher, *Genocide* CD liner notes.

21. *Behind the Music: Judas Priest*, VH1 television, 2001.

22. Bryan Reesman, *Metalogy* CD liner notes.

23. *Metal: A Headbanger's Journey.*

24. *Behind the Music: Judas Priest.*

25. Gett, p. 25.

26. *Behind the Music: Judas Priest.*

27. Garry Sharpe-Young, "Call for the Priest. K.K. Downing Opens up on Some of the Lesser Known Passages in the Band History," *Rockdetector*, March 3, 2006, <http://www.rockdetector.com/interviews/artist,33344.sm?id=80> (December 3, 2007).

28. Wright.

29. *Electric Eye* DVD liner notes.

30. Wright.

31. Geoff Barton, *Essential Judas Priest* CD liner notes.

Chapter 4. Unleashed

1. *Heavy: The Story of Metal*, VH1 documentary, 2006.

2. Ibid.

3. Ibid.

4. *Sin After Sin* CD liner notes.

5. Robert Palmer, "Angel, Judas Priest and Godz, Rock Groups, Play at Palladium," *The New York Times*, March 12, 1978.

6. *Stained Class* CD liner notes.

7. Jon Young, "Judas Priest," *Trouser Press*, June 1978, *Rock's Backpages*, <http://www.rocks backpages.com/print.html?ArticleID=9594> (November 28, 2006).

8. Ibid.

9. Ibid.

10. Rob Halford, *Fresh Air* radio interview, June 21, 2005, *NPR: National Public Radio*, <http://www. npr.org/templates/ story/story.php?storyId=4712606> (December 5, 2007).

11. *Heavy: The Story of Metal*.

12. Ibid.

13. Ibid.

14. Don Snowden, "Judas Priest in Santa Monica" *Los Angeles Times*, October 25, 1979, *Rock's Backpages*, <http://www.rocksbackpages.com/print.html?ArticleID=8387> (November 28, 2006).

15. *Unleashed in the East* CD liner notes.

16. *Classic Albums—Judas Priest, British Steel*, Eagle Eye/Pioneer, 2001.

17. *British Steel* CD liner notes.

18. *Classic Albums—Judas Priest, British Steel*.

19. Ibid.

20. Ibid.

21. Ibid.

22. Ibid.

23. Ibid.

24. "British Steel," *Judas Priest Info Pages*, n.d., <http://members.firstinter.net/markster/BRITISHSTEEL.html> (November 30, 2007).

25. J. Kordosh, "Judas Priest: Hell-Bent for Eagle Scout-Hood?" *CREEM*, August 1981, p. 29.

26. Bryan Reesman, *Metalogy* CD liner notes.

27. Jeb Wright, "Ian Hill of Judas Priest," *Classic Rock Revisited*, 2002, <http://www.classicrockrevisied.com/interviews02/ian_hill_interview_2002.htm> (July 30, 2007).

28. Kordosh, p. 29.

29. *Screaming for Vengeance* CD liner notes.

30. *Behind the Music: Judas Priest*, VH1 television, 2001.

31. Wright.

32. Steve Huey, *All Music Guide*, 4th Edition, Vladimir Bogdanov, Chris Woodstra, and Stephen Erlewine, eds. (San Francisco, Calif.: Backbeat Books 2001).

33. Joe Fernbacher, "The Further Adventures of Judas Priest and the Flivver of Doom," *CREEM*, November 1982, p. 55.

34. "Screaming For Vengeance," *Judas Priest Info Pages*, n.d., <http://members.firstinter.net/markster/SCREAMINGFORVENGEANCE.html> (November 30, 2007).

35. *Classic Albums—Judas Priest, British Steel.*

Chapter 5. Defending the Faith

1. Steve Gett, *Heavy Duty* (Port Chester, N.Y.: Cherry Lane Books, 1984), p. 63.

2. Richard Hogan, "The Judas Priest 'Defenders' Quiz," *Circus*, May 31, 1984, p. 67.

3. Bryan Reesman, *Metalogy* CD liner notes.

4. Jon Pareles, "Debate Spurs Hearings On Rating Rock Lyrics," *The New York Times*, September 18, 1985, <http://select.nytimes.com/search/restricted/article?res=F70913FF3C5D0C7B8DDDA00894DD484D81> (January 20, 2008).

5. Ibid.

6. Ibid.

7. Ibid.

8. "Judas Priest," *CREEM Magazine Presents Metal Hall of Fame 1987*, p. 41.

9. Sylvie Simmons, "Judas Priest, Leathered, Studded Dudes Or . . ." *CREEM*, September 1986, *Rock's Backpages*, <http://www.rocksbackpages.com/print.html?ArticleID=6865> (November 28, 2006).

10. Ibid.

11. "Judas Priest," *CREEM Metal Hall of Fame 1987*, p. 41.

12. Steve Gett, "Loving Metallian," *CREEM Metal*, January 1985, p. 32.

13. *Turbo* CD liner notes.

14. *Ram It Down* CD liner notes.

15. Larry Rohter, "2 Families Sue Heavy-Metal Band As Having Driven Sons to Suicide," *The New York Times*, July 17, 1990, <http://query.nytimes.com/gst/fullpage.html?res=9C0CE0D71E30F934A25754C0A966958260> (December 5, 2007).

16. "Nevada's High Court Allows Suit on Rock Band's Lyrics," *Reuters*, August 26, 1988, <http://query.nytimes.com/gst/fullpage.html?res=940DE2DE1238F935A1575BC0A96E948260> (December 5, 2007).

17. Rohter.

18. Ibid.

19. Rob Halford, *Fresh Air* radio interview, June 21, 2005, *NPR: National Public Radio*, <http://www.npr.org/templates/ story/story.php?storyId=4712606> (December 5, 2007).

20. Rohter.

21. "Nevada's High Court Allows Suit on Rock Band's Lyrics."

22. Jon Pareles, "Pop View; Speed-Metal: Extreme, Yes; Evil, No," *The New York Times*, September 25, 1988, <http://query.nytimes.com/gst/fullpage.html?res=940DE1D91130F936A1575AC0A96E948260> (December 5, 2007).

23. Ibid.

24. Halford *Fresh Air* radio interview.

25. "Judas Priest's Lead Singer Testifies," Associated Press, August 1, 1990, <http://query.nytimes.com/gst/fullpage.html?res=9C0CE1DA143FF932A3575BC0A966958260&sec=&spon=&pagewanted=print> (December 5, 2007).

26. "Band is Held Not Liable in Suicides of Two Fans," *Reuters*, August 25, 1990, *Reverse Speech*, <http://www.reversespeech.com/backwards.htm> (December 5, 2007).

27. Ibid.

28. *Painkiller* CD liner notes.

29. Jon Pareles, "Pick an Evil. Any Evil. And Then Scream," *The New York Times*, December 17, 1990, <http://query.nytimes.com/gst/fullpage.html?res=9C0CE4DE153FF934A2 5751C1A966958260> (December 5, 2007).

30. *Painkiller* CD liner notes.

31. Rob Halford, *Rockline* radio interview, December 11, 2006.

32. Neil Daniels, *Judas Priest: Defenders of the Faith* (London: Omnibus Press, 2007), p. 138.

33. Bryan Reesman, "Rob Halford: Beyond the Realms of Digital," *Metal Edge*, March 2007, p. 9.

34. Jon Pareles, "Visions of the Apocalypse With a Touch of Melody," *The New York Times*, January 19, 1994, <http://query.nytimes.com/gst/fullpage.html?res=9406E3D61730F93 AA25752C0A962958260> (December 5, 2007).

35. Ibid.

36. Daniels, p. 141.

37. Chad Bowar, "The Glenn Tipton Interview," *About.com*, n.d., <http://www.heavymetal.about.com/od/interviews/a/glenntipton.htm?p=1> (December 5, 2007).

38. Ibid.

39. Glenn Tipton, *Edge of the World* CD liner notes.

40. Daniels, p. 142.

41. Ibid., p. 145.

42. Andrew C. Revkin, "A Metal-Head Becomes a Metal-God. Heavy," *The New York Times*, July 27, 1997, <http://query.nytimes.com/gst/fullpage.html?res=9901E0D8133BF 934A15754C0A961958260> (December 5, 2007).

43. Ibid.

44. Ibid.

45. *Behind the Music: Judas Priest*, VH1 television, 2001.

46. Revkin.

47. Daniels, p. 152.

48. "Rob Halford Discusses Sexuality Publicly For The First Time," *MTV News*, February 5, 1998, <http://www.mtv.com/news/articles/1429870/19980205/story.jhtml> (December 3, 2007).

49. Ibid.

50. Ibid.

51. "Judas Priest Speaks About Rob Halford's Sexual Openness," *MTV News*, February 19, 1998, <http://www.mtv.com/news/articles/1429869/19980219/halford_rob.jhtml> (December 3, 2007).

52. Halford *Fresh Air* radio interview.

53. Ibid.

Chapter 6. Judas Rising

1. David Lee Wilson, "Interview With Judas Priest's Glenn Tipton," *KNAC.com*, March 12, 2002, <http://www.knac.com/article.asp?ArticleID=540> (November 30, 2007).

2. Orpheus, "Interview with Tim The Ripper Owens of Judas Priest," *Metal Temple*, May 19, 2001, <http://www.metal-temple.com/interview.asp?id=29> (December 3, 2007).

3. Arion Berger, "Judas Priest: *Demolition* CD review," *Rolling Stone*, August 30, 2001, <http://www.rollingstone.com/artists/judaspriest/albums/album/

274281/review/6068203/demolition> (December 3, 2007).

4. Steve Baltin, "Judas Priest's Real-Life Rock Star," *Rolling Stone*, September 20, 2001, <http://www.rollingstone.com/news/story/5933195/judas_priests_reallife_rock_star> (December 3, 2007).

5. *Behind the Music: Judas Priest*, VH1 television, 2001.

6. Orpheus.

7. Andrew Dansby, "Judas Priest Forge New Steel," *Rolling Stone*, July 23, 2003, <http://www.rollingstone.com/news/story/5936738/judas_priest_forge_new_steel> (December 5, 2007).

8. Rob Halford, *Fresh Air* radio interview, June 21, 2005, *NPR: National Public Radio*, <http://www.npr.org/templates/story/story.php?storyId=4712606> (December 3, 2007).

9. Dansby.

10. Jon Wiederhorn, "Judas Priest Discusses Emotional Reunion, Leaving Ripper Owens Behind," *VH1.com*, July 15, 2003, <http://www.vh1.com/news/articles/1473785/20030714/ judas_priest.jhtml> (December 6, 2007).

11. Ibid.

12. Ibid.

13. Ibid.

14. Adem Tepedelen, "Ripper Returns in Iced Earth," *Rolling Stone*, March 31, 2004, <http://www. rollingstone.com/news/story/5937008/ripper_returns_ in_iced_earth> (December 3, 2007).

15. Ben Ratliff, "Ozzfest Trudges On, Laden With Sponsors and Politics," *The New York Times*, July 16, 2004, <http://query.nytimes.com/gst/full page.html?res=9A04E1DC143AF935 A25754C0A96 29C8B63&partner=rssnyt&emc=rss> (December 5, 2007).

16. Soft Boy, "Ozzfest 2004," *Metal Express Radio*, n.d., <http://www.metalexpressradio.com/ menu.php?main=reviews&id=717> (December 3, 2007).

17. Jon Wiederhorn, "Judas Priest Have No Problem 'Letting The Metal Roar Out' On New LP," *MTV News*, September 2, 2004, <http://www.mtv.com/ news/articles/1490731/ 20040902/judas_priest. jhtml> (December 3, 2007).

18. Andrew Dansby, "Judas Priest Teach 'Metalogy,'" *Rolling Stone*, February 12, 2004, <http://www.rollingstone.com/artists/judaspriest/ articles/story/5937212/judas_priest_teach_metalogy> (December 6, 2007).

19. Ibid.

20. Wiederhorn, "Judas Priest Have No Problem."

21. Jon Wiederhorn, "Judas Priest Reborn with *Retribution*, Revisit Classic Sound," *VH1.com*, February 18, 2005, <http://www.mtv.com/news/

articles/1497270/20050218/ judas_priest.jhtml>
(December 6, 2007).

22. Ibid.

23. Dom Lawson, "Steel Warriors," *Kerrang!* magazine via JudasPriest.com, n.d., <http://www.judas priest.com/review/default.asp> (July 5, 2007).

24. Wiederhorn, "Judas Priest Have No Problem."

25. Edgar Leoni, *Nostradamus and His Prophecies* (Mineola, N.Y.: Dover Publications, 2000), p. 16.

26. Ibid. p. 559.

27. Ibid. p. 564.

28. John Wiederhorn, "Judas Priest's Nostradamus Concept LP: A Heavy-Metal 'Phantom of the Opera,'" *VH1 News*, June 29, 2006, <http:// www.vh1.com/artists/news/1535473/ 20060629/ judas_priest.jhtml> (November 30, 2007).

29. Ibid.

30. Bryan Reesman, "Rob Halford: Beyond the Realms of Digital," *Metal Edge*, March 2007, p. 5.

31. Press Release, "Judas Priest Roar Back with an Instant Epic, 'Nostradamus' on Multiple Classic Formats and a World Tour," June 9, 2008.

32. *Heavy: The Story of Metal*, VH1 documentary, 2006.

33. Ibid.

Concert Tours

1. "Albums," *Judas Priest Info Pages*, n.d.,<http://www.jpinfo.tk> (December 10, 2007).

FURTHER READING

Books

Brunning, Bob. *Heavy Metal.* Grand Rapids, Mich.: Peter Bedrick, 1999.

Feinstein, Stephen. *The 1970s from Watergate to Disco.* Berkeley Heights, N.J.: Enslow Publishers, Inc., 2006.

Hayes, Malcolm. *1970s: Turbulent Times.* (20th Century Music series.) Milwaukee, Wisc.: Gareth Stevens Pub., 2002.

Popoff, Martin. *Judas Priest: Heavy Metal Painkillers—An Illustrated History.* Toronto, Ontario: ECW Press, 2007.

Schaefer, A.R. *Forming a Band.* Mankato, Minn.: Capstone High-Interest Books, 2004.

Ung, Rod. *Heavy Metal Techniques for Lead Guitar.* Australia: Koala Publications, 1997.

Weinstein, Deena. *Heavy Metal: The Music and Its Culture.* New York: Da Capo Press, 2000.

Internet Addresses

Judas Priest
http://www.judaspriest.com

Judas Priest
http://www.mtv.com/music/artist/judas_priest/
   artist.jhtml#bio

INDEX